Dedicated to all the security leaders working hard to protect their company. I hope this book helps you disconnect from work and connect with your family. Special thanks to my children Lily, Ben, and Sonora who helped design the characters in this book.

First Edition, 2024
"Chief Information Security Officer"
© 2024 by Christian Hyatt
All rights reserved.

No part of this book may be reproduced, stored, or transmitted without permission from the author or publisher.

Created in collaboration with Timmy Bauer
Produced and Published by Dinosaur House
Art by Dinosaur House, a kids book production studio
Lead Artist: Alejandra Moreno

DINOSAUR HOUSE
We Turn Industry Leaders into Kids Book Authors

www.DinosaurHouse.com

Chief Information Security Officer

By Christian Hyatt

Once upon a time, in a very normal house, at a very normal bedtime, Dad was tucking his kids into bed. Their family dog, CISO the German Shepherd, was laying peacefully on the rug.

Dad began telling the kids a bedtime story. And as he did, his kids entered a world of imagination, one where CISO, their dog, was a hero.

"Do you know what CISO stands for?"

"Chief Information Security Officer"
"Wait a second, that's what you do!"

"Yes, but in this story, it's CISO's job!"
risk3sixty
PC
CISO needed to protect all the computers, diaries, and private stuff for the citizens of Secure City and the workers of its biggest company: **Power Corp**.

"Protect from who, dad?"

"Good question", dad said, and as he answered, his voice turned sinister...

"From the evil, villainous, and corrupt..."

Hamster Hackers!

"Oh no!"

SPOOF

- height: 5 centimeters
- weight: 95 grams
- Super Power: Able to trick people
- Weakness: Very poofy, cannot go near vacuums

HEY PARENTS, DID YOU KNOW?

Email spoofing is a technique used in email phishing attacks to trick users into thinking a message came from a person or entity they know or trust. So, if you ever see a suspicious email from friends or family asking you to send them money - it might be spoofing!

PHISHER

- Height: 12 centimeters
- Weight: 60 grams
- Superpower: uses a grappling gun to shoot hooks
- Weakness: Afraid of Crowds

HEY PARENTS, DID YOU KNOW?

Phishing is a cybercrime in which a target is contacted by email, telephone or text message by someone posing as a legitimate institution to lure individuals into providing sensitive data such as personal information, banking and credit card details, and passwords.

DOX

- Height: 15 centimeters
- Weight: 65 grams
- Superpower: Lazer eyes
- Weakness: Allergic to lettuce

HEY PARENTS, DID YOU KNOW?

Doxing or doxxing is the act of publicly providing personally identifiable information about an individual or organization, usually via the Internet and without their consent.

RANSOM

Height: 6.8 centimeters

Weight: 70 grams

Superpower: Super speed

Weakness: Sick if she comes near onions

HEY PARENTS, DID YOU KNOW?

Ransomware is malware that employs encryption to hold a victim's information at ransom until a fee is paid. In 2017, more than 230,000 computers were impacted by the WannaCry Ransomware attack. The estimated loss was more than $4 Billion.

"The toughest Hamster Hackers you've ever met."
"You see, the job of CISO, is to be a guardian against digital crimes and invasions."
risk3sixty
"Invasions!?!"
"Crimes!?!"
"Like what?"

Like stealing hard drives out of video games systems!

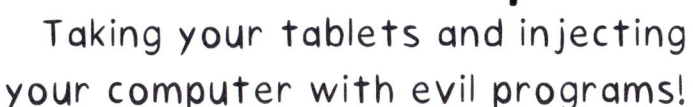

Taking your tablets and injecting your computer with evil programs!

Stealing all the pictures off of your phones!

Even breaking into Power Corp and shutting off the power to Secure City.

It was a bleak world now.

Everything the citizens of Secure City owned had been hijacked!

The only things to do were boring things like watching history documentaries and doing homework.

All the phones had viruses.

None of the tablets were working right.

All the tvs only had the news.

But fear not, because CISO knew what to do.

While the Hamsters thought they had taken control, CISO was gathering a team of specialists to handle the problem.

He was now more determined than ever to restore security and happiness to the citizens.

In the dimly lit operations room of Power Corp, CISO assembled his own team of cybersecurity heroes!

"Pups, assemble!"

There was Cypher the Cat, an expert in encryption.

Firewall Foxhound, who could build defenses faster than anyone.

Backup Beagle, who always made sure important systems had duplicates.

Restoration Rottweiler, who could rebuild things from the ground up.

Antivirus Airedoodle, who could detect and eliminate invasions.

CISO's team gathered in the operations room, scanned the map, identified the villans patterns and planned their next move.

CISO located the threat and came up with a plan to defeat the evil Hamsters and secure the city again.

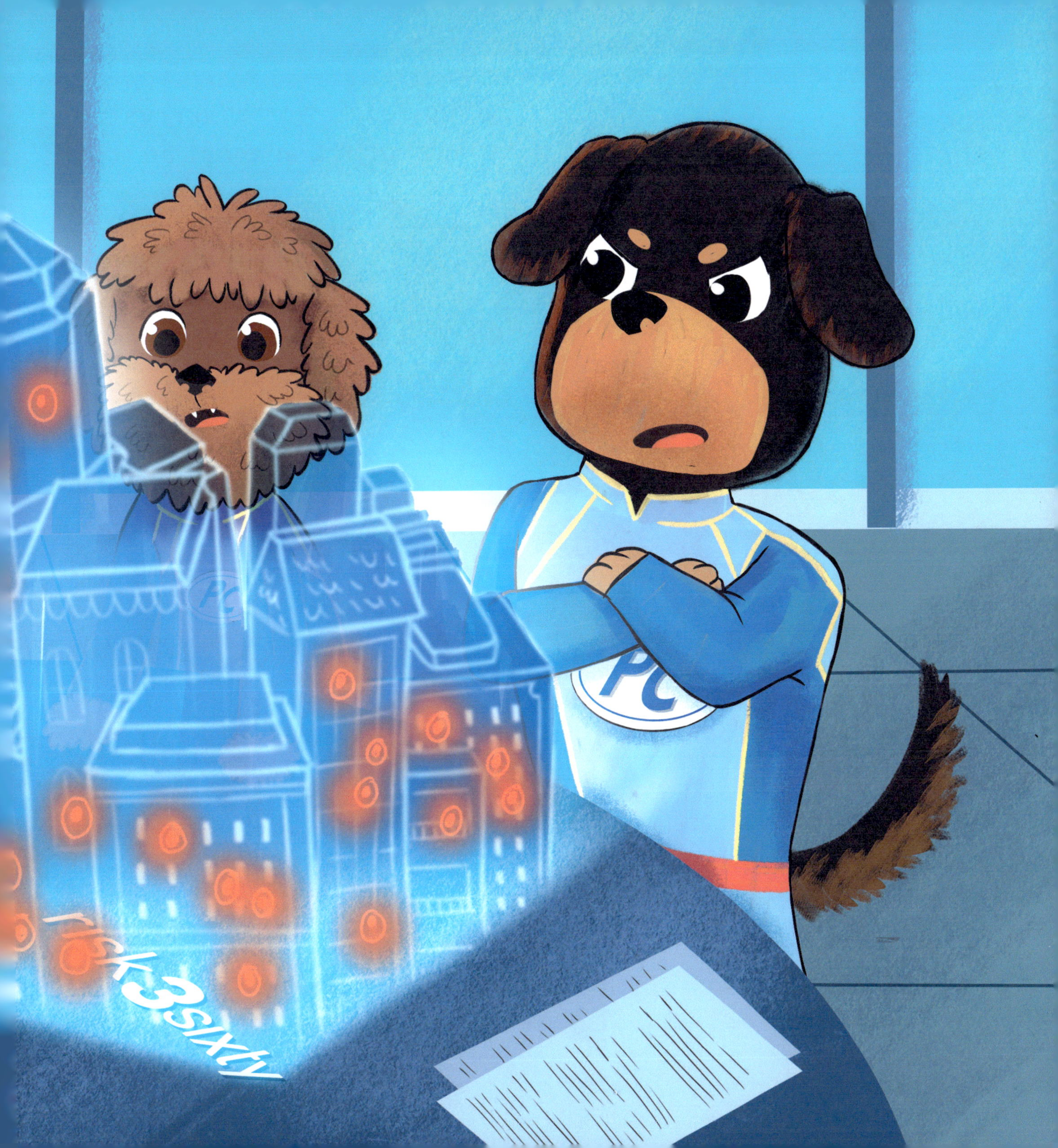
risk3sixty

Backup Beagle worked on restoring as much of the internet he could,

while Firewall Fox would secure the perimeter and make sure the Hamsters couldn't get back in.

They decided that CISO and Cypher would go on the offensive to the Hamster Hackers' hideout and recover the stolen digital treasures.

The Hamsters were so distracted celebrating their victory by watching the tragic events happening around the city, they didn't see CISO coming.

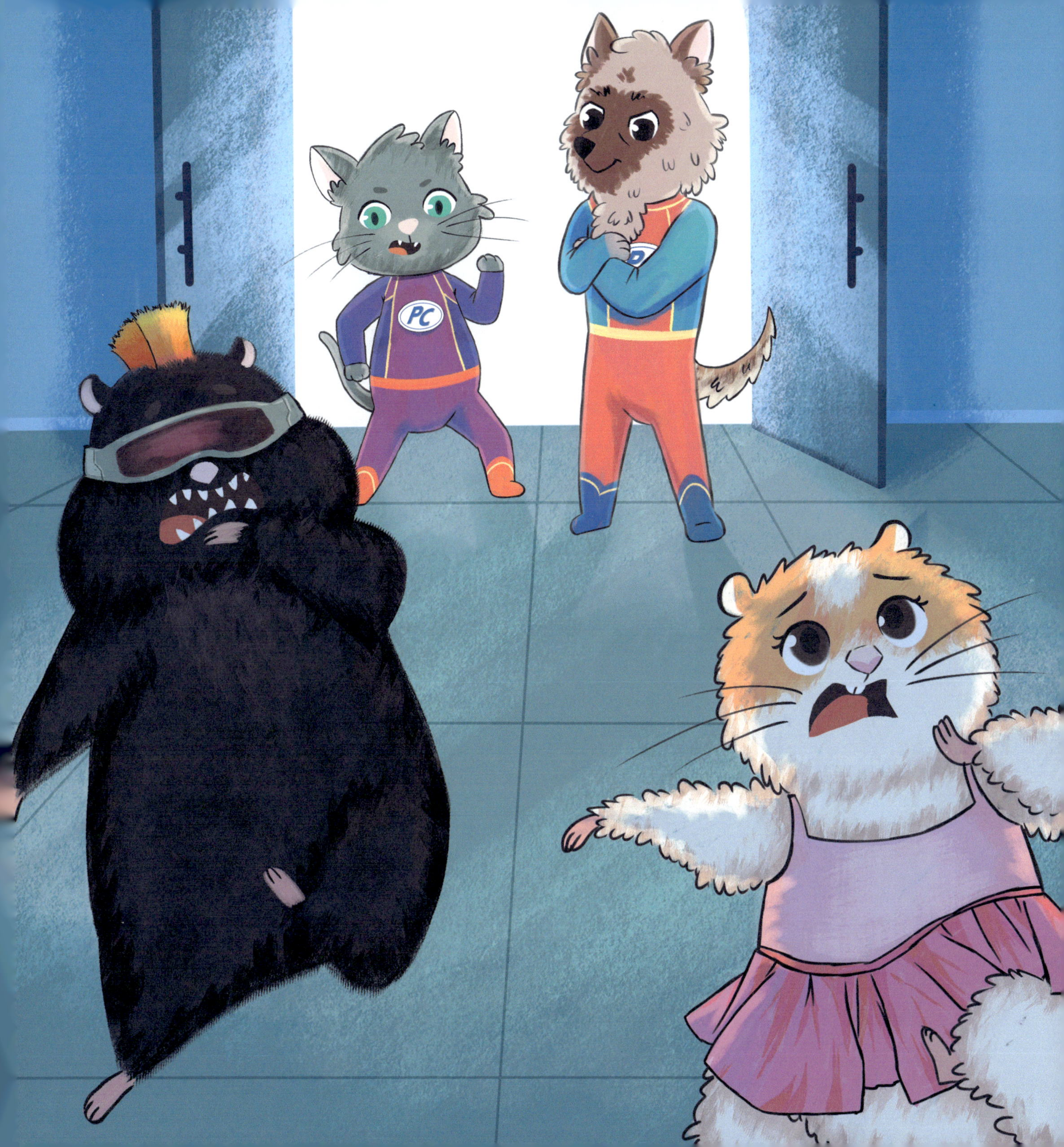
PC

It's time for an epic cyber security battle!

note: dramatization, this is not exactly how real cyber security work is done.

With the Hamsters defeated, CISO's team got to work recovering and restoring.

They returned every stolen game, photo, and video back to its rightful owner.

The joyous reactions of the city filled the air with laughter, happiness, and security!

SECURITY LEVEL: super high

CYBER CRIME: super low

Dad ended the story with a smile, tucking his kids into bed.

"And that, my little cybersecurity experts, is how CISO saved Secure City."

The kids were now filled with dreams of adventure.

CISO, the family dog, stirred from his spot on the rug, as if he knew he'd been the star of tonight's bedtime story.

And in the quiet of the very normal house, at a very normal bedtime, a very special bond between a dad, his kids... and their dog, was formed.

THE END.

→ **WHAT DID YOU LEARN ABOUT THE JOB OF A CISO?**

　　A: They love making soups
　　B: They are great leaders
　　C: They don't like technology

→ **ARE HAMSTER HACKERS REAL?**

→ **CIRCLE THE THINGS THAT COULD BE STOLEN BY HACKERS:**

Furniture
Computer files
Phone pictures
Passwords
Helicopters

Cheeseburgers
Email accounts
Bank accounts
Gold coins
Digital coins

Download the **free** coloring pages here:
www.risk3sixty.com/ciso-the-dog

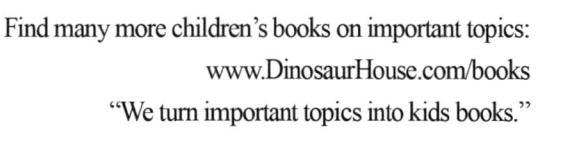

Find many more children's books on important topics:
www.DinosaurHouse.com/books
"We turn important topics into kids books."

DINOSAUR
HOUSE

Made in the USA
Columbia, SC
15 February 2025